RESPONSIBILITIES OF THE OBSESSED

RESPONSIBILITIES OF THE OBSESSED

GORO TAKANO

BLAZEVOX[BOOKS]
Buffalo, New York

Responsibilities of the Obsessed by Goro Takano
Copyright © 2013

Published by BlazeVOX [books]

All rights reserved. No part of this book may be reproduced without the publisher's written permission, except for brief quotations in reviews.

Printed in the United States of America

Interior design and typesetting by Geoffrey Gatza
Cover art: *Dynamics* by Yu Shiotsuki

First Edition
ISBN: 978-1-60964-117-7
Library of Congress Control Number: 2012948140

BlazeVOX [books]
76 Inwood Place
Buffalo, NY 14209

Editor@blazevox.org

publisher of weird little books

BlazeVOX [books]

blazevox.org

BlazeVOX

Acknowledgments

I offer my grateful acknowledgment for the support of the editors of the following printed/online publications, where the poems in this book first appeared:

"Blast" --- *My Postwar Life: New Writings from Japan and Okinawa* (Chicago, IL: Chicago Quarterly Review Books, 2012) edited by Elizabeth McKenzie

"Seven Dreams, Seven Nights" and "Imprisoned: A Renshi" --- *Contemporary World Literature* edited by Sam Hamod (http://contemporaryworldliterature.com/?s=goro+takano)

"That Thing: A Noh Script" --- *fourW twenty-two* (Wagga Wagga, NSW, Australia: fourW Press, 2011) edited by David Gilbey

"What I May Imagine When I Die" --- *fourW twenty-three* (Wagga Wagga, NSW, Australia: fourW Press, 2012) edited by David Gilbey

"The Colon Girl" --- "A Selection of Contemporary Poetry from Japan" in *Big Bridge* edited by Jane Joritz-Nakagawa (http://www.bigbridge.org/BB16/features/japan/japangtakano.htm)

"Doggone" --- "'If I didn't write it down, it's shhhhh': On Writing Dementia" in *EOAGH* edited by Susan M. Schultz (http://eoagh.com/?p=1581)

"The Remains of Remains" --- *Catamaran Literary Reader Vol. 1* (Santa Cruz, CA: Catamaran Literary Reader, 2012) edited by Catherine Segurson, Elizabeth McKenzie et al.

"A Buried Ode," "A Mourner in a Library," "A Camel and a Camera," "Appearances and Disappearances," "Tanka: I Am," "Midnight Rainbow," "Pudding," "Tanka: A Man and His First Newborn," "A Woman Full of Water" and "With One More Step Ahead" --- *With One More Step Ahead: A Novel* (Buffalo, NY: BlazeVOX, 2009), which was my first novel (Note: All those poems appeared in the novel exclusively as the works by its protagonists)

Contents

Blast 11

About You 18

Seven Dreams, Seven Nights 20

Imprisoned: A Renshi 23

DJ Wake's Radio Lonelyhearts 30

That Thing: A Noh Script 32

The Colon Girl 37

What I May Imagine When I Die 41

Doggone 43

The Remains of Remains 44

A Buried Ode 49

A Mourner in a Library 53

A Camel and a Camera 56

Appearances and Disappearances 59

Tanka: I Am 64

Midnight Rainbow 67

Pudding 74

Tanka: A Man and His First Newborn 76

A Woman Full of Water 78

With One More Step Ahead 83

Responsibilities of the Obsessed

Blast

Did you forget your last night's dream? Again?

Don't worry, it is right here. Read it and remember:

In the dream, you're an obese Japanese novelist with a heavy case of senile dementia, who has no idea when a story you've been writing recently will be completed.

And, in the dream, your story (tentatively titled *Extravaganza*) is somehow about America. However, you don't remember what the story is all about anymore.

In fact, you don't remember your name and age. You don't even remember who I am. All you remember is that you're writing an extraordinary story.

Now you bump into the twenty-somethingth writer's block. You still don't know how to transcend it.

So you choose to take a rest. You sit on a living-room sofa and start to watch TV. A pile of fancy-looking chocolate-bar wrappers is on your table, right in front of you. And your chin and lower lip are left smeared with mud-like chocolate. Of course, as usual, you don't care at all.

Your child, a newborn baby, is sleeping next to you, soundly on a hippo-shaped cushion on the sofa.

Your sex-maniac spouse is not present. It is a benefit now for you neither to know where (s)he is nor to remember who (s)he is anymore. Otherwise, you might try to kill him or her.

If you could lose all your words, it might be another benefit. However, you still cannot. Because your dementia is not heavy enough? Because you're such a coward? Who knows?

Anyway, only you and the baby are in the scene. It may be morning, afternoon, or night. You try to forget about your manuscript for a while. You just imagine your obese body floating in the water, with your eyes, ears, nostrils, and nothing else above the surface.

Your room is on the top floor of a tall building, which seems to be located in the center of a nameless city. Through a large window, you can see the spring sunrise, the summertime thunderhead, or the winter moon.

A woman appears on the TV.

She says she is a lecturer on Creative Writing. "Poor you, cannot start a new paragraph? Okay, I'll show you an intriguing exercise," she says. "Pick up five different words from all the paragraphs you've written so far, and make a new story out of all of them within a minute. Don't think. Rather, let your fingers think. Believe me, that will be the very next paragraph your story needs now!"

Following her advice, you pick up intuitively "sex," "heavy," "transcend," "extraordinary," and "hippo." And, while hearing your baby's gossamer-like breathing, your fingers begin to write the following lines on a piece of paper:

> *An extraordinary hippo transcends heavy sex*
> *Heavy sex promotes a cute idea*
> *A cute idea fires a tainted castle*
> *A tainted castle invites a horny mouse*
> *A horny mouse kills a handsome Japanese*
> *A handsome Japanese visits a shabby nation*
> *A shabby nation colonizes the entire world*
> *The entire world ignores an individual soul*
> *An individual soul discovers a handy hideout*
> *A handy hideout welcomes a lonesome thief*
> *A lonesome thief meets an American maiden*
> *An American maiden dedicates a bogus prayer*
> *A bogus prayer occupies vacant space*
> *Vacant space encloses an extraordinary hippo*

What a bunch of crap. What is this lecturer thinking about, you ask the TV monitor.

When you are about to dump the paper, the same woman turns to you again on the screen, with a frown on her face:

"Didn't this practice work at all? Alas, sorry about that. Then why don't you forget all you've written until now and start from scratch? Of course, you definitely need a good intro for a brand-new story, don't you? The next exercise will be so effective, believe me, that you can get it right now, just quick. All you have to do is to transform the following Grimms' tale in the way your fingers wish it to be. Not in the way your brain wishes, mind you. I'm pretty sure the end result will function perfectly as the ideal beginning of your new work!"

There was once a poor woman who had two little girls. The youngest was sent to the forest every day to gather wood.

Once when she had gone a long way before finding any, a beautiful little child appeared who helped her to pick up the wood and carried it home for her.

Then in a twinkling he vanished. The little girl told her mother, but the mother wouldn't believe her.

Then one day she brought home a rosebud and told her mother the beautiful child had given it to her and said he would come again when the rosebud opened. The mother put the rosebud in water.

One morning the little girl didn't get up out of bed. The mother went and found the child dead, but looking very lovely. The rosebud had opened that same morning.

Staring at the TV screen, you find your fingers hovering in the air, as if to scribble on an invisible piece of paper something you have never been able to discover by yourself:

Right after the Pacific war, in a small local city, there was once a poor old Japanese woman who had two young beautiful girls. The younger one was sent to a shady bar downtown every night to entertain teenage American GIs. She always admired every American soldier, regardless of his skin color. "Gibu mi chokoreito, GI" was a vogue phrase among a majority of hungry street kids at that time. And all Japanese men looked simply too skinny, too miserable, and still too male-oriented to the girl. So she wanted to marry an American GI someday. That was her only wish.

Once when she had worked until midnight before finding any ideally good-looking GI in the bar, a beautiful young American soldier appeared. He said to her, in the way even she could understand, "No sex, I'm okay, only talk, TALK."

Then in a twinkle he vanished. The girl told her mama-san boss, but she wouldn't believe her.

Then one day she brought to the boss a box full of expensive-looking chocolates and told her the beautiful guy had given it to her and said he would come again when she ate up all of them. Secretly, the mama-san brought the box back home and gave it to her illegitimate daughter whose American father had already abandoned his Japanese family and headed back home. Naturally, the illegitimate daughter ate them all up.

One morning the young girl didn't come to the bar. The mama-san boss stopped by her shabby house, and the girl's mother found her dead, but looking very lovely. That same morning some playful GIs set the bar on fire under the influence of alcohol, and it was closed down. And, that night, another box full of expensive-looking chocolates was delivered there.

What a fool's errand. Boy, this gets nowhere, you sigh.

"That's all for today. Thanks for watching, see you tomorrow," the lecturer says. You pull out a remote from under the hippo-shaped cushion and tune the TV to the next channel.

Suddenly, a man starts to preach on the screen.

For some reason, he appears faceless and bodiless. Only his hands are clearly illuminated by spotlights. Another camera shows a horde of people bowing to him in unison. He may be a kind of god, but you don't know what kind of religion he leads. And you remember, yes, remember, that he is what you have been waiting for.

You find yourself gazing at his stature in wonder. You stand up, and, without hesitation, make a deep bow to the television.

During his sermon, the man on TV lifts up a naked newborn baby, composedly, from behind the pulpit. Sandwiching its torso between his large palms, he extends both of his arms horizontally, as straight as he can.

"Folks, imitate me," he shouts. "If you are watching this program on an upper floor of a hotel or an apartment or whatever, along with your baby like this one, go up to a window, open it right away, and stick him or her out of it, just like this. And, only with your arms straight, hold your adorable baby safely in the air."

Holding your sleeping baby in your arms, you approach the large window like a marionette.

"If you can maintain this posture at least for an hour," the preacher shouts again, "it will prove clearly that your heart is full of true, pristine, parental love. If you should drop your baby, your carelessness will show clearly what kind of person you are at this moment. And I'm always here for a person like you."

You open the window. Timidly, you look down. On the street, the head of every occasional passerby looks merely like a grain of sand.

Tension mounts rapidly in your entire system.

Sandwiching the baby's torso between your palms, you face the outside landscape.

Raising your courage, you extend both of your arms horizontally, as straight as you can.

And you whisper to yourself: "I'll show you how much I love you."

Now, your newborn is sleeping soundly in midair, supported only by your two arms.

You're still keeping this posture. The preacher said "at least for an hour." So, only five minutes to go. You're sweating from every pore.

"I'm stupid, I know I am," you mumble to the sleeping baby. Two minutes to go.

Suddenly, a gale of wind blows hard. The newborn wakes up, and begins to cry fretfully.

"Stop it," you say impatiently. "Cannot you see what I'm doing? Do you want to fall down?"

The baby doesn't stop crying. Another gale of wind blows. One minute to go.

Just one more minute, and your love will be clearly proved. "Stop crying, you bastard," you shout.

And your baby starts to fall down.

During its freefall, it metamorphoses into a nuke.

A few seconds later, an unimaginable blast erupts from the street, and you kneel down, as if to pray. The whole outside landscape vanishes, and only your building is miraculously left unscathed.

The TV shows the preacher leaving the pulpit with his black suitcase in his hand, amid the standing ovation of his followers. And, as the volume of the cheers begins to lower, a commentator's indifferent voice cuts in:

"Can you see where the baby he was holding is now? It is a lifelike doll, in fact, its name is Rosebud. It is now in his suitcase, perfectly disjointed."

You have never been so absent-minded before. Of course, you cannot remember where you are, who you are, what you were doing.

"I'll have you remember that," someone says behind your back, and you turn around mechanically.

"This is my very first time at Ground Zero," your publisher says with a grin. "How are you today? Do you still remember who I am? Did you eat up the whole box of fancy chocolates I brought to you last time? You did, didn't you? Not to worry, I'll bring you a new box of them next time."

You say nothing. All you can do is to just imagine your obese body floating in the water, with your eyes, ears, nostrils, and nothing else above the surface. Just like this cushion, you say silently to yourself.

"How's your *Extravaganza* going, by the way? Are you still having writer's block? Well, just as I expected," the publisher says, and takes something out of his black suitcase.

"Use this package again. How many did I give you so far? Twenty-something, maybe. Now you can put all the parts together by yourself, right? Make this doll the last one, will you? Otherwise, you would be too much addicted and reach the point of no return. Got it?

"Plus, here is what you have long wanted. A list of available nationalities," the publisher adds, tossing a pile of documents onto the exact place on the sofa where your baby was sleeping. "It goes in alphabetical order. Today you're Japanese, so tomorrow you must be, let's see, Jordanian, I guess. Double-check the list by yourself, and get ready by the next time we meet, okay?"

This must be a dream, you say to yourself, holding the package in your arms. The publisher bursts into laughter. "How do you know this is a dream? Can you really figure out what a true dream is like? Do you remember, for instance, your last night's dream?"

You say nothing again.

"Don't worry, it is right here," the publisher says.

And you, the obese novelist with a heavy case of senile dementia, are led smoothly to the next blast.

About You

The following is what will surely happen to you right after you finish reading this prose poem. That is, a kind of prophecy for you.

Before going into its details, you should first know a bit about the true situation you're in. "Oh, no thanks," you may say, "I know all about me, already." Unfortunately, however, you don't anymore.

Now you're awfully aged and a heavy case of senile dementia. Your whole understanding of yourself is nothing but your delusion. All the individuals you see as your family, lover, friends, and colleagues are nothing but strangers for you. You've already lost the entire memory of your age, sex, nationality, address, workplace, and everything else.

Now, let's return to the "prophecy."

After reading this poem, you'll say to yourself: "Bollocks! Who can dare to call me a horrible case of dementia? No kidding, please!" And you'll look around to see your family, lover, friends, and colleagues again. To your surprise, you'll find all of them completely frozen to the ground, exactly in the same posture as before you started reading this poem. So will be all clocks and watches, and there will be no more sounds. Feeling as if you're stuck in the middle of a perfect vacuum, you'll be tremendously terrified.

Just like a typical murderer who escapes pell-mell from the scene of his (or her) crime, you'll toss this poem away and start running to a nearby square where you can be quickly lost in a crowd. You'll never know that it is the typical beginning of a SD patient's sleepwalking-like roam.

All people in the square will be, of course, frozen to the ground. So will be every car and motorcycle and bicycle, every wind and cloud, every animal, and the sun. Only you and the falling snow will be in motion. Coldness will be so harsh that you cannot help wringing your body. "I can still twist my body this much, because I'm still young and healthy. 'Awfully aged'? Give me a break," you'll shout. The delusion is that deeply rooted in you.

Through the blizzard, you'll discover in the center of the square a huge bulletin board saying: "NO WORRY, LADIES AND GENTLEMEN! NO EVIL HUMAN BEING EXISTS IN

THIS NATION! EVERYBODY KNOWS YOU'RE THE MOST PEACE-LOVING PEOPLE ON EARTH."

Totally at a loss where to go, you'll start roaming again, with a terrible shudder. After a long aimless journey, you'll come back to the place where you're reading this poem now. Its door will be wide open, but some mysterious force will prevent you from striding the threshold. So you'll peep inside and find another you right there. Finishing reading this poem, this another one will shout: "My decision was finally made. From now on I'll discard my family, lover, friends, and colleagues. I'll even have my entire genital organ cut away. And I'll devote the rest of my life offering the true peace of mind to every evil-minded stranger living outside of this nation. Every one of them will be my adopted child. For this sacred aim, I'll happily sacrifice the future of my own family, my own country, and my own race!"

Yet, once this another you stands up and tries to get through the open door, his (or her) face will turn suddenly pale in front of you. "IT'S WIDE OPEN, BUT I CANNOT PASS THROUGH IT! WHY?" His (or her) useless struggle will start desperately before you. You'll have to hear his (or her) refrain-like sick moan: "Is this eternal house arrest? If so, will I starve to death before long?" And you can no longer stand staying there.

So you'll attempt to return to the same square, whispering to yourself: "The author of that awful 'prophecy' must be still hiding there. I'll spot and kill him right away, or her, with my own hands!"

Of course, your rage is justifiable. But you'll never attain your goal, because you, the awfully heavy case of senile dementia, won't remember how to return to the square. Your fruitless roam will have to go on forever, with no memory of what you've done and what you're doing.

Last but not least, you have to know now that it is you who wrote this prophecy. Unfortunately, though, you cannot even remember it anymore.

Seven Dreams, Seven Nights

A stranger comes to me and
    asks me   on his knees: "Tie me up, mister,
NOW"
When I try to ask him about his crime   this dream grinds
    to a brief halt

                              Then

A huge book is left forgotten   in an
    immense desert   and
    it is nothing   but me
    A wind blows   I open   All
    the pages are   just blank

                              Then

Every time TV says   "The next breaking news   is this"
another sorrow is dodged   Nobody poses this question
anymore: "When will this
sorrowful dodge   cease?"

                              Then

Now my survival   relies solely on
    the fresh   gills around my

        neck
So I dive into   water
Who can assure me
that I won't   get drowned in this dream

                                Then

Millions of ants are sleeping   in a ragged ant hill   which is
       me   As the dream
    weathers
                               I weather
        at the same pace

                                Then

A
hypocrite
is
sharpening
his
own
tongue
on
a
whetstone
I
wake
up
there
and
start
cutting

off
my
own
And
I   wake up again

                              Then

            A
            mad
            woman's
            will
            is
            in   my   hand:
            "Only
            the
            unseen
            is
            your
            subject
            matter"
Her
            shadow
            passes
            through
            a
            barrier
            of
            this
            dream   and
vanishes

                              Then

Imprisoned: A Renshi

[Verse 1]

A brand-new tooth was born in my mouth
at age 44.

The dentist said,
"Welcome to a land of milk and honey, mister."

"A land? The land!" I chuckled.
He ignored my correction and added:

"You'll soon have two more heads,
two white wings, a vagina, and more —
But don't get near electricity,
or you'll lose all possibilities imaginable."

Then he undressed and showed his pregnant belly.

The bill was too criminal to pay,
not covered by medical insurance.

With no other choice left,
I became one of his concubines.

[Verse 2]

I disappeared, because I was unjustly arrested
I'm still imprisoned because I'm a poet and "dangerous"
My only companion in jail is a sturdy male peacock

In court I was often called a deadly "terrorist"
The media billed me daily as a pathetic "poemist"
"Just like Plato's *Republic*," I sighed and the peacock nodded

I've been long fasting since the day of my arrest
Everyday I'm busy contemplating the infinite
So I don't feel hunger, thirst, the heat, nor cold

When I'm electrocuted the peacock will spread its tail
on which countless suns will reflect my "tragedy" again
What a Hamlet I am — What a Quixote I am

[Verse 3]

The days of my poetry-loving grandfather
who went missing in action as an imperial-army grunt
on foreign soil in 1945
are finally numbered in my hometown Hiroshima

He keeps motionless in his bed
with numerous IVs and catheters all over his body
I sit beside him to tell him a bedtime story
　「どうして英語なんか使う？鬼畜の言葉だぞ」, he grumbles

I tell him about my shadow's recent arbitrariness
Every morning it declares, "Fuck the entire world!"
and leaves me behind
Every evening it hangs on me and slobbers,
"All the murders in human history are my fault"
　「それがおまえの詩か？実相観入がまだ足らんな」, my granddad grumbles

　「さあ、いよいよ今日だ・・・光あれ」, he shouts and changes into a large larva
Its shell splits straight open and a massive firefly looms up
My shadow sneers at my body dressed with IVs and catheters
And I whisper,
　「もの思へば沢のほたるもわが身よりあくがれいづるたまかとぞ見る」

[Verse 4]

Now, in an immense and quiet crematorium
You're trying to pick up with long chopsticks
a tiny bone of the Adam's apple
out of a bed of the hot ashes sheeting
the cremated corpse of your loved one
And you know an Adam's apple is
called a "throat buddha" in Japanese

What would you do next if this was your true story?

Your story shouldn't be clear
Your story shouldn't be about any personal matter
Your story should be authorless
Your story should be timeless
Your story should be misunderstood in many ways
Your story's characters should be mere signs
Your story should exist to disembody the whole world

If you believe firmly that
you can remember easily the voice
of the ocean you heard before with your loved one
when you drop the "throat buddha"
into the bottom of a tiny porcelain urn
in the immense and quiet crematorium
you may have to start all over again

[Verse 5]

And today, when I'm about to take a walk
the walk suddenly refuses to be taken
"This is not my walk of life anymore,"
it says with a strong-minded look

The walk snatches from my hand a book
The title: *Everything That Rises Must Converge*
"Now is my turn to read this book by Flannery O'Connor,"
the walk says and swiftly starts to pack

The title of the book comes from the freak
evolutionism established by
a French-born philosopher who believed
that everything must develop to God's peak

Fearing this cruel division, I phone an ark
The walk is now on the way to rising to the spot
called by the philosopher the "omega point"
The phone is still ringing hollow and blank

[Verse 6]

A kindergarten is a block away from here
Right behind it is a dead flower garden
A beer garden is two blocks away
Right behind it is a graveyard
A lost child is giggling there alone

Millions of small handouts start falling from the sky
Each one of them says: "Surrender and die, otherwise you must live more"
Eeny Meeny Miny Mo, the lost child mumbles
Eeny Meeny Miny Mo, everybody else mumbles
"A big storm is coming," the weather forecast announces

So I disjoint my limbs
And unplug my eyes and ears
And turn on the shiny respirator
Which is you, my sweetheart
Three cheers for artificial intercourses

[Notes]

The following glosses are for the Japanese parts in the third verse of this "renshi"-like poem:

--- First Japanese line: "How come you use English? That's the goddamn devil's language."

--- Second Japanese line: "Is that your poetry? You need more 'explorations into essentials.'" The expression "explorations into essentials" is a phrase coined by the tanka poet Saito Mokichi (1882-1953).

--- Third Japanese line: "Today is the day --- Let there be light."

--- Fourth Japanese line: "While contemplating / I see a firefly in mountain streams / as if it is a soul wandering / out of my own flesh." This is a waka poem from the poetess Izumi Shikibu, born in the late tenth century.

DJ Wake's Radio Lonelyhearts

Hello deejay Wake. I love your talk show, I really do. You started this great program when I was born and you've kept going on the air ever since. So let me ask you this big favor. Hope you won't mind spreading your faithful listener's word about this top secret to the entire world.

Today, the tiny place I'm living in now, a no-name locality on the periphery of this big country, finally declared independence. You want to know its present population? Well, in fact, just five of us (me included). And we all are sleepers, in fact. I mean, we completed this bloodless revolution while sleeping deeply.

We haven't obtained, unfortunately, any official acknowledgement from UN or any other nation yet. Moreover, nobody in your big country has noticed our quiet riot yet. None of our ex-fellow countrymen know that, a while ago, we five grabbed fifty hectares of forest in this remote wasteland, the one isolated by high mountains from your homeland, for this successful disobedience to the longstanding autocracy in which they're (and you're, too) still repressed unawares.

They still believe innocently their country free, because the repression is too efficiently calculated for them to disclose by themselves. Some oppositional forces exist, yes, but they will never be let win there and their angry voices will never be sincerely negotiated. Did you know that the autocrat's one and only gulag for dissents had been hidden deep in the forest which is now ours? We escaped from it by sleeping it away, took to the streets in our dream world, got back to the forest last night and occupied it peacefully. Let me warn you, deejay Wake: If you believe that living in your big country is what life should be all about, I would say that such a life is already outdated.

Here, let me introduce all my four comrades to you: the first one gave birth and joy to me; the second one gave sickness and anger to me; the third one gave age and sorrow to me; and the fourth one gave death and pleasure to me. They all appear rather mummified, but they are my eternal home now.

Our nation-founding motto is very simple: "Trust is everything here, but nothing there." Shortly, in this land of promise, we'll start establishing from scratch our new social welfare system, healthcare system, water and food self-sufficiency system, mass media, and education. We'll also start exploiting the natural resources hidden in this forest, and discussing how to conserve the necessary energy. National security and anti-terrorism measures will be also at the top of our agenda. We'll be so busy from now on that we'll have far less time to sleep. And, yes, we'll also have to proclaim our own Constitution immediately.

Right after reading this letter, you may shout to the mike: "Jeez, what an outcast of the universe!" Oh, your yell will sound just like an echo of mine from the high mountains. But we know what's truly on your mind, deejay Wake. You want to join us, right? Longing to immigrate here asap, right? Go into exile now, and we can hire you as a spy or our minister of foreign affairs. Give thought to it, will you?

Ah, your show is really awesome. You're always there without any break, every night and day, all the year around. How come you can keep talking like that, without any sleep? Why did you get such an alias? Wasn't that my own name?

I'll surely write to you again, if I can remove mountains. Otherwise, this letter will be the last from me, the unattended bedridden with haunted mind. More power to every aged sleeper! Ciao now, my dear deejay.

That Thing: A Noh Script

[waki]
Again the bell sounds at the Sekidera temple
Everything is evanescent, people often say
But it does not make any sense to my aged ears

> [shite]
> After all
> I could not tell you exactly then
> what it was that fell suddenly on me from the sky

[waki]
Like a fallen tree long buried underground
Like pampas grass with no chance to come into ear
I have been hiding myself from the entire world
But my mind is a seed and my word is a flower
I may win back a new flow
If my passé color gains momentum again

> [shite]
> Am I still regretting it?
> Yes, maybe I am
> I'm still wishing I could have told you clearly
> about that thing's true identity
> by my poetry's main force

[waki]
The sand on the seashore may disappear someday
But the words on my tongue will not, definitely not

> [shite]
> Oh no, I know I'm now deceiving myself
> Am I really wishing that way now? Hell no
> I didn't want to tell you about that thing then
> and I still don't

I will never tell you about whether it was liquid or powdery or solid
whether it was strangely lukewarm or murderously freezing
whether its color was gray or silver or transparent
and what the first letter of its name was

[waki]
Oh what a pity, in old days
all the inns where I stayed overnight with my past lovers
were decorated with shiny tortoiseshell
Their hedges were hung with crafted gold flowers
Their doors were studded with sparkling crystals
And their beds were always longing to see us
hiding ourselves under their gorgeously embroidered covers

[shite]
To be honest, I didn't want to describe that thing in words
I'll never do that, never and never, I was repeating to myself

HEY WHAT ARE YOU MUMBLING NOTHING IS FALLING FROM THE SKY STOP FOOLING YOURSELF AND TAKE OFF YOUR SMELLY CLOTHES QUICK WILL YOU AREN'T YOU HUNGRY AGAIN LIKE A WOLF HUH NOW COME CLOSER I'LL SHOW YOU A COLLECTION OF MY OLD LPS LET'S DIG SOME OF THEM OKAY I'LL GIVE YOU ENOUGH PETTING AS ALWAYS THAT'S ALL YOUR WITHERING BODY WANTS RIGHT I'M NOT ONLY YOUR MAN BUT ALSO YOUR MASTER AND FOOD SO OPEN YOUR LEGS HEY OPEN WIDER SURRENDER EVERY PIECE OF YOU TO ME AND SHOW ME THE BEST OF YOUR EROS NOW

[shite]
When you vanished from my sight I couldn't recognize it
Since then I've died my own death numerously
But I remain the same somehow

And since then
every time I breathed that thing came into my nostrils or mouth
every time I walked on the road that thing lay beneath my steps
every time I moved my hands that thing touched them arbitrarily
every time I raised my voice that thing spoke instead of me

I was a geocentric-theory woman
You were a heliocentric-theory man
A long time ago
I often believed that your sins were all mine
and promised myself to put all yours on my tender shoulders
But ah but

I KNOW THAT EVERY ITALICIZED STANZA IN THIS POEM IS ORIGINALLY FROM THE JAPANESE NOH PLAY *KOMACHI AT SEKIDERA* IT IS YOU WHO QUOTED ALL OF THEM ISN'T IT ALSO I ALREADY KNOW THAT EVERY KEYWORD OF MY CAPITALIZED SPEECHES IN THIS POEM IS ORIGINALLY FROM EMMANUEL LEVINAS'S *TOTALITÉ ET INFINI* YOU STOLE ALL OF THEM FROM HIS PHILOSOPHY WITHOUT PERMISSION DIDN'T YOU I STILL REMEMBER BOTH OF THE WORKS WERE YOUR FAVORITES I CAN EVEN PREDICT THAT YOU WILL SOON CITE AUDACIOUSLY THE LYRICS OF A FOLK MUSIC I USED TO WHISPER EVERY DAY IN MY CHILDHOOD ITS TITLE WAS AHHH LET'S SEE AHHH YES NOW I REMEMBER IT WAS CALLED THE ICE CREAM SONG

WHAT THE HECK DOES SHITE STAND FOR WHAT THE HELL DOES WAKI MEAN ANYWAY STOP THIS WHOLE NONSENSE RIGHT NOW WHY DON'T YOU GIVE UP YOUR STUPID PET STYLE FOR A CHANGE AND WRITE A TOTALLY BRANDNEW POEM FOR GOD'S SAKE HOW COME YOU PROMISED YOURSELF TO KEEP REVISING ETERNALLY THIS WEIRD CORPSE OOPS NOT CORPSE SORRY BUT OPUS FINISH THIS CRAZY PIECE ASAP AND COME GRAB MY HARDENED CROTCH NOW QUICK

[shite]
Why do I have to be a woman
Why do you have to be a man
I may be a man and you may be a woman
Or both of us may be male and female
Or both of us may be women and nothing else

[waki]
You say you're a centenarian
And Komachi as we know her must be still alive
She has to exist somewhere in this world

So undoubtedly
You must be the ruined Komachi we've been looking for

> [shite]
> So inevitably
> my masturbation is repeated from its beginning
> totally possessed
> without cease
> just like whirling in the air
> And again
> my odorless urine starts to leak

OH NO KIDDING WOMAN HOW COME YOU CAN TELL SUCH A STUPID LIE IT SMELLS YOU HEAR ME SMELLS SO BAD AND A BIT TOO SLIMY FOR URINE

> out of my familiar diaper
> uncontrollably and ill-manneredly

WHY DIAPER ALL OF A SUDDEN YOU'RE NOW WHOLLY NAKED LOOK AT YOURSELF

[waki]
Ahhh, hundred years of a butterfly's dance
on a full-blown flower, with no companion around

HERE LET ME SING THE ICE CREAM SONG FOR YOU ice cream ice cream oh my beloved i won't leave you nohow so behave nicely again YOU DON'T CARE WHETHER I'M ALREADY DEAD OR STILL ALIVE DO YOU NOW DUMP THIS ABSURD VERSE AND LOOK AT MY FACE CANNOT YOU SEE IT'S REPLETE WITH INFINITY HUH THAT'S WHAT YOU HAVE BEEN LONG LOOKING FOR ISN'T IT NOW LOOK AT ME HEY LOOK

[waki]
Leaning on her old stick
she staggers down to her straw-made hut
So this centenarian witch is
nobody but the ruined Komachi
nothing but her final act

WHO IS KOMACHI WOMAN SCREW YOU ALL YOU'RE SAYING HERE IS SIMPLY RIDICULOUS TO ME ISN'T THAT YOUR PENNAME OR SOMETHING HOW MANY TIMES DID I TELL YOU TO STOP SUCH NONSENSE TONIGHT IS STILL YOUNG SO DON'T DRESS YOURSELF YET OKAY YOU'RE STILL HUNGRY FOR THAT WILD THING HUH VERY VERY HUNGRY AREN'T YOU

The Colon Girl

When a CCD camera enters the entrance of his aged colon, an unknown naked girl appears dimly in a 3D imagery on the monitor positioned in front of the old poet.

Don't pretend to forget me, she says, and shows her vagina to him.

You forgot to cut your middle finger's nail, so it injured me right here in bed last night, she says, and he starts wondering whether she is pointing at her pubic region or his own stretched anus.

His face draws up at the weird pain, and the doctor says with a grin, "Are you a colonoscopy virgin? No worries, the whole thing will be done like a flash."

While the fiberscope creeps along, the pristine girl straddles it as if she rides on a carousel and shouts a line from *The Catcher in the Rye*, which is the old poet's favorite:

"I'm sort of glad they've got the atomic bomb invented. If there's ever another war, I'm going to sit right the hell on top of it."

"Look, this is your rectum. Seems clean and healthy," the doctor says.

Do you remember, the girl asks, what you said in bed? "Everybody in this world is a stolen child, every family tie is a sham, and every stranger can be your kin," you said. She chuckles, while he is still afraid of cancer.

The camera turns right and shows numerous damp folds on the monitor.

"I don't want to drink tap water anymore," a nurse says to her colleague in the next room.

"Oh, are you afraid of the radiation leak? Come on, it is not at the dangerous level yet," the colleague says.

The nurse grimaces and says: "I don't buy that. The radiation adds up. Nothing so threatening like the quake-hit nuclear power plant."

The old poet ponders how many times the tap water has run over those rolling folds.

Ah, my whole body smells like a laxative, the girl says, and starts romping again, pinching her nose.

The old poet closes his eyes, and feels the girl taking a shower in the dark.

Do you still believe, she asks, that a moderation of good produces likewise a moderation in evil? You said so last night, even mentioning Anthony so-and-so's excess of virtue, she adds.

He vaguely remembers telling someone about St. Anthony of Egypt somewhere in the distant past: "If the monk had stayed at home and attended to his sister, no devils would have plagued him."

Now may be the time for you to be plagued, goody-goody, she adds.

His eyes open again, and see the CCD moving slowly into the transverse colon. "So far so good," the doctor says.

The old poet stares at his middle fingers.

The fiberscope pushes forward further, and the darkness in the old poet is revealed one after another.

The girl is getting bigger and older on the monitor, and he cannot imagine any longer how further she can grow.

Now dressed up just like the radiation-fearing nurse, she peeps back into the CCD, and asks him why he didn't look into her eyes in bed.

He cannot reply.

I still miss you so much, she says and asks again: You know why?

The old poet answers, "WHO ARE YOU, ANYWAY?"

At the same time, though, he somehow feels as if he knows this 3D mature woman beyond time and space.

Now, to the old poet, the doctor seems to have told him a bloody lie. This colonoscopy goes on and on like an eternity, and, on the contrary, the earth's age seems so momentary.

The fiberscope finally descends into the ascending colon, discovering no polyp whatsoever.

I still miss you, the girl-turned-hag says while bouncing listlessly on the slimy walls, because you're just like a vacant house in my neighborhood, at which I have gazed idly, since my earliest recollections, out of my bedroom window every night.

The old poet tries to ask the doctor what time it is, but somehow cannot ask clearly.

I don't know who lived there, and I don't care why they all had to run away under cover of night, she continues. Yet, gazing at the house every night, I've gradually found myself imagining so realistically their old happy days, their lovely smiles, their clean laundry, their joyful dinners, and their peaceful sleep. I don't know who they are, but, due to this weird habit of watching the vacancy, I still cannot stop feeling as if an important part of me has disappeared with those complete strangers.

Suddenly, pointing at the monitor, the radiation-fearing nurse mumbles to the doctor: "Isn't this a polyp, Tony?"

The hag hides completely behind the millimeter-size lump.

If you want to remove this, she whispers, remove me with it, my beloved Holden Caulfield!

Looking closely at the 3D imagery, the doctor still wonders whether it is benign or malignant.

The final decision is simply beyond the old poet.

He closes his eyes again, and dimly notices the demolished nuclear power plant in the pitch-darkness.

It's just like me, he thinks.

And feels the earth shake.

And feels the whole colon tremble.

Ah, I think I'm beginning to know what time is truly like, he says to himself and finally opens his vacant eyes again.

What I May Imagine When I Die

from dawn to another dusk
your lust shines again
like a noctiluca
and is answered silently
by mine, an eye for an eye

sucking at each other's
saliva, alternately,
we reconfirm
how frivolous our
being still is

my finger reaches
the nothingness of the muffled
bottom of your whole
and reflects, finally,
a slimy light of lunacy

while you permeate
my flesh and
overflow
golden down dances on
your eyes, so madly

while, heated up,
I turn slowly
into a cloud of gas
you get condensed to
delay my silly leak

now I can see
on your sweaty bare back
the back of a lost soldier
too much starved to
stop his cannibalism

vanish now, you
with my name who wonders about
the meaning of this embrace
and come here quick, pleasure,
and make this moment simply vague

a beheaded king
of the castle standing
out on my ruined cerebrum
is weathered on your skin now
what a pandemonium

moonlight mutes
our colors, when we squirm
like two myriapods
copulating mechanically
right under dead leaves

my fang to yours
we tear the cocoon of
each other's soul
and, by another sunrise,
we finish molting

Doggone

With a razor in his hand, someone approaches you from behind. You don't know who he is, but he seems to know you from time immemorial. The strange man tells you not to turn around. He also tells you to open your tightly-shut wrinkled eyes. You don't understand him at all, but you obey his order. He slits one of your eyeballs slowly, and a jello-like substance oozes out of it. Before you respond dodderingly, the man says that you're now in an airport. You don't understand him again. I'm just a hack novelist, mister, you say to him. I'm still young and vigorous, mister --- I think I can keep writing still more, but people say I've already written too much pulp literature for too long --- almost all my life, they say --- and they warn it's high time for me to write my last novel titled *A Basket Case* --- everybody is nuts --- just a bunch of untrustworthy narrators, you continue, clicking your mossy tongue. No matter what you write, brother, you cannot create your own destiny at all --- the strange man says. Anyway, welcome to this midnight airport, he also says, while walking slowly away from your back. Your flight schedule has been just messed up so far, brother --- if you don't want to miss another connecting flight just as you have done before, you should run and rush to the ticket counter over there --- the strange man shouts from afar. You don't understand him again. This is my house, mister, not a goddamn airport, and I'm now relieving myself in this closed toilet --- you shout back without looking back, just as you were told. Why don't you look down, brother? --- the strange man's distant voice echoes in your ears. No matter what you have as your own, the echo continues, you cannot fly without that tiny holy book down there. You look down, and find a fresh passport left casually right under the toilet bowl you're sitting on. You wonder whether or not it is your last novel. Forget your own power and pray, brother, just pray for your peaceful return --- your own crumpled mouth whispers simply like the strange man. Plenty of ants are crowding around the jello-like stuff on the shiny floor. You wish you could scoop it up and flush it with your own stool, but your decrepit hand cannot find the flush bar anymore. You look up, and discover an inaudible airplane passing in the pitch-black sky over a cathedral-like terminal. Ah, what a new day, you say to yourself and notice no more toilet rolls left. What a crock, you sigh. While wondering whether you're about to faint, you restart relieving yourself.

The Remains of Remains
(Inspired by Flannery O'Connor and Keijiro Suga)

At your favorite café you are about to order another cup of coffee, while reading a huge philosophy book.

The café is located in the center of a city with a mundane name that starts with the word "New."

Inside, a number of fluorescent lights are glaring.

The page you've been reading so far explains a wacky religious principle that every human being needs to be a prey to unexpected violence to receive ultimate revelation.

You've been reading this mosaic hardcover to write a book in the near future --- a book about yourself.

When, putting the book on your table, you try to ask for a waiter, an aged, barefoot hobo-looking man opens the door.

Huddling in some layers of rugged overcoats and wearing a couple of soiled scarves, he walks quietly into the café, which is far cooler due to the air-conditioning than the outside.

The café is now quite crowded, and all the customers (except you and a mother and her baby sitting at the farthest corner from you) are a bunch of beautifully dressed, sexually attractive, aristocratically handsome men and women.

In your eyes, though, they all look like fancy-looking mannequins neglected in a summer house.

You say to yourself, "These snobs never stop longing for other people's property and feeding on the anger of others, while I'm not like them."

You can neither see the young mother breastfeeding her baby nor hear her singing a tranquil lullaby.

On your table, beside the philosophy book, there is a pile of medications and a diary riddled with your everyday punctual entries on your own temperature, blood pressure, body fat percentage, pulse rate, et cetera. "Hospitals are my enemy," you say silently.

With a thick book tucked under his arm, the hobo, with a deeply wrinkled face, begins to walk very slowly among the crowd.

He seems to be looking for an empty space, and the only untaken chair in the café is right in front of you.

He must be a mongrel seasonal worker or something. "He is nothing but the exotic," you even emphasize in your mind.

Nobody else casts a glance at the hobo, and he keeps dragging his feet among them silently, like --- your imagination begins to twist up --- just like an ancient haiku poet traveling alone from one place to another.

You start supposing that this haiku poet must have been born in so many places that he hasn't obtained any roots.

You say to yourself he probably used to be, say, in Patagonia, Nebraska, New Mexico, and Alaska. He used to live, sometimes, in adobe pueblos, surrounded by micaceous windows, or stay in a tiny village on a mesa. He even used to walk barefoot through so many deserts, so many ice fields, vast tundra, immense plains of alabaster, the horizon of nothing but minerals, and endless-looking wasteland.

You visualize a world map and continue mumbling one place-name after another, ignoring every other customer's threatening gaze.

"I don't want to go native here," you swear once again in your mind.

After departing from, say, Tibet, the haiku poet must have whispered some haiku and forgotten them quickly:

Beyond a wave	Of motorcycle beeps	A monk's whisper
Candlelight fades	No wind enters the pagoda	The echo of a gong
A god in the dark	Stares at me, I look down	I'm not enough yet

Now you wonder why the hobo's asymmetric dark eyes keep avoiding the only empty chair positioned before your eyes.

As if he slides languidly on water without any map in hand, the hobo keeps going around in the cafe, now with the thick book right on the top of his head, while moving all his fingers lightly in the air, as if he caresses something like a keyboard.

WHERE DID MY LAND GO? The hobo whispers, but you cannot hear it.

He must be a roaming pianist or something, you say to yourself. Playing, say, *The Goldberg Variations*, perhaps. This lunatic may be now looking for the best-suited chair for his invisible Steinway. And such a chair must be unlike the one right here.

WHY CANNOT YOU LEAVE ME ALONE? The hobo whispers again, but you cannot hear it, either.

Again, you start supposing that the languages used by the chosen few like this pianist are now in danger of extinction. "To save them, he probably needs some alien help like me," you conclude secretly.

SO MANY VOICES AT A TIME ALWAYS DRIVE ME CRAZY, the hobo whispers again, but it eludes you just the same.

You wonder what kind of landscape will be left in his mind's eye at the end of his life.

And you have yet to wonder what kind of soundscape will echo in your ears at the end of yours.

His eyes finally meet yours, as if a predator and its prey exchange a momentary dialogue of death.

You keep in your bosom a solemn question to ask him, but cannot help feeling it's already known to this reticent old man before voicing it.

WE HAVE TO CUT DOWN ON OUR NUMBER AND SIMPLIFY OURSELVES, OTHERWISE, the hobo shouts suddenly.

The shout is quickly muffled, though, by the buzz of the crowd in the cafe, for instance:

"Did you know that the notorious cesium 137 never perishes from the earth?"

"Yes. We can move it from one place to another, but cannot extinguish it."

You begin to suppose that the hobo might once have been exposed to a massive dose of radiation.

Under a number of fluorescent lamps, you visualize him thinking: "I'm dirtied, but I'm too old to regret it. But what if my body dirties the lands of others and the purity of children?"

The buzz of the crowd continues yet:

"Why are you still hesitating to evacuate?"

"That's exactly what I was about to ask you!"

"How long can we enjoy this electricity?"

THIS IS THE REMAINS OF REMAINS, the hobo shouts again like a ghost.

And --- his fingers start groping an invisible woman's bosom in the air.

Or --- they start rubbing an invisible man's penis in the void.

Until the intangible milk starts to drop or the intangible semen begins to splash, you continue to watch his whole movement as if you were a tourist.

His hostile eyes meet yours again, when you are about to open your mouth at last and ask him:

"Don't you think our nostalgia is sometimes dangerous? The more strongly we expect our homeland to be the same as before, the more violently we may deprive others on it of their independent stories about their ongoing changes. Don't you think so?"

In the midst of your question, the hobo's sinewy hand throws the thick mosaic hardcover (titled *Human Development*) like a cannonball and it strikes home on your forehead.

What if that's the same philosophy book you've been reading so far?

YOU MIXED-BLOOD GHOST, I'LL TRAVEL YOU NEXT, the hobo mumbles, and a frontier in your soul moves.

Deep sky-blue pink, heavy mass of wind, barren richness, overwhelming light, blood-red soil, and the whole universe on fire at sunset.

The young mother's lullaby finally reaches your ears:

On looking up, on looking down,
She saw a dead man on the ground
The worms crawled out, the worms crawled in
Then she unto the parson said
Shall I be so when I die
O yes O yes the parson said
You will be so when you are dead

The hobo opens the door and leaves, probably for another place you've never seen.

When your sight begins to collapse, the owner of the café declares that the closing time has come.

No more cups of coffee for you, obviously.

A Buried Ode

> *Please come here yesterday*
> *Please come back here at this time of yesterday*
> *And see my yesterday's face*
> *Because I am always in yesterday's world, always*
>
> *--- from* "Please Come Here Yesterday" *by Muroh Saisei*

Son, forgive your father's silliness.
When you were about to be pushed somehow
out of your mother's womb in this tiny delivery room,
all of a sudden,
your father found himself unable to stand watching your bloody appearance.
To the doctor shouting "Push!,"
your father said in an extremely low voice, "Excuse me,"
and went out of the room
and got out of the hospital and
stopped by a national cemetery near it.
The whole world was dawning gradually around him.
Nobody was in the cemetery except him.
While you were about to be pushed out,
your father started to dig a hole on a vacant ground
surrounded by plenty of tombstones.
Only with both of his hands.
Your father didn't know why he had to dig like that.
But he couldn't help it.
Your father dug, dug, and kept digging,
sweating silently, right under a cerise sky.
Why did he turn his back on your coming to this dawning world
and choose suddenly to walk away?
Why was he suddenly afraid of blood?
Yes, your father was digging, while your mother was pushing you out.

While he was digging, your father was closing his eyes
and visualizing the color of the blood covering all your newborn flesh.

That must be the color of truth, he thought.
Or the color of faithfulness. Or the color of selflessness.
Or the color of responsibility. Or the color of love and sincerity.
Or the color of guiltlessness.
Oh, I'm a sinner, your father groaned.
He had hated to become a father throughout his whole life.
His primary wish had been always to live only for himself.
I'm a goddamn selfish, faithless, irresponsible, insincere, loveless,
guilty human being, your father thought and ground his teeth.
I'm not yet qualified at all to shoulder such a bloody bond,
he confessed to himself.
Then your father started to shout to the bottom of the hole, "Why?"
Why did he choose to create your flesh and blood?
Why did he agree so carelessly to your mother's desire to be a mother?
"Why?" He shouted and dug, alternately.
His lonesome voice sank into the hole, along with drops of sweat from his face.

The entire world was beginning to shine.
But your father didn't dare to look at it.
He was still closing his eyes and digging quietly,
feeling as if he had been tunneling his way into himself.
The hole got deeper and deeper.
His hands were simply black with mud.
Then an old woman's voice gradually loomed up to his ears from the deep.
To your father, it sounded like his own grandmother's voice.
Maybe right, maybe wrong. Anyway, it was the voice of somebody's grandmother.
She was apparently whispering alone about her late husband,
closing her eyes on her bed and rubbing slowly her aged, contracted, stiffened body.
Your father listened while digging.

When we got married, that war had not started yet, the old woman whispered.
Yes, a long time ago.
The first time I met him, he was working in my father's small factory.
And I was coming down with tuberculosis
and lying on my bed everyday like now, she whispered.
All of a sudden, he came to inquire after me, with a big living fish in hand.
This is a carp, he said. Its blood is good for tuberculosis, he also said.
My parents agreed and let him into my bedroom.
Beside me, he chopped out the carp's head into a metallic bowl

and poured its blood into a small cup.
Drink this, he insisted. I hate blood, I said.
My parents left the bedroom to throw away the carp's carcass.
He suddenly held the blood in his mouth and kissed me.
The blood was pushed out from his lips, and dug its way into my throat.
Into the darkness inside my body.
Just as if I had been gulping his own blood.
One more time, please, I said. Before my parents come back here, I said.
He kissed me again and again. I got all the blood from his mouth.
My lips looked probably like a vagina delivering a baby.
The carp's blood saved my life.
And he said later, "That carp is, in fact, what I painted ---
It slipped out of my painting, but
I happened to recapture it. I was lucky. And so were you."

In those days, dating in public was regarded as embarrassing, she whispered.
The war was approaching rapidly,
and sacrificing one's loyalty to our nation for loving someone particular was
seen as an unforgivable unpatriotic indulgence.
So, before our marriage, we used to date always at dawn,
hiding ourselves in the nearest graveyard.
One day, he dug a hole somewhere in the graveyard,
shouted something into its bottom, and buried it quickly with his muddy hands.
I asked, what did you shout? A kind of ode to you, he said.
Tell me, I insisted.
No, our truth should be silent in our time and
my ode should be kept buried here until I die, he said.
And, a year later, he was drafted as a grunt and killed on foreign soil.
He sacrificed his blood for our nation.
Maybe he had to kill some foreign people and
sacrifice their blood for his own sake and feel terribly guilty and traumatized.
A day after I got the news
that he had been pushed out to the enemy's pitch-dark jungle to be killed,
I wandered, with my baby on my back, with my nipples dripping milk,
along with the fading memory of the carp's blood falling from his lips,
in the graveyard demolished entirely by the enemy's air raid.
Yes, just to dig out his buried voice.
But I couldn't find where it was, she whispered.
Now I am buried like him, waiting for someone to dig up my voice.

No happiness without blood, she whispered.
Then your father heard every tomb whispering in chorus with the aged woman.
No happiness without blood.

Son, your father kept digging and digging,
with morning sunshine on his head.
No happiness without blood, he kept mumbling alone.
He didn't understand what it really meant.
His whisper kept dropping into the hole.
Then he finally stopped digging,
because he noticed his own murmur almost overflowing the hole.
He climbed up to the ground and began to bury the hole.
Once it was buried completely, he came back to this tiny delivery room.
Your mother is still pushing and pushing,
and your bloody head and shoulders are coming out.
Son, I'll never walk away from this room anymore.
I'll be watching your birth until the end.
If circumstances permit, I may even dare to lick your bloody body clean.
I may even dare to hold in my mouth the placenta having protected you so far.
I know that's a silly idea, but less silly than the way I used to be.
All I want to say now is thank you, son. I thank you, thank you, and thank you.
You're like a piece of ode to me, coming up from the deep to tickle my heart.
I wish you to try someday, hopefully after I die, to dig up my silly ode to you,
which will remain buried down there.

A Mourner in a Library

> *Then Fate o'errules, that One Man holding Troth,*
> *A Million fail, confounding Oath on Oath.*
> *--- Robin Goodfellow, from Shakespeare's* A Midsummer Night's Dream

The last time I came across her was a week after she died.
In my university library, right on its basement floor.
I'm a graduate student now. Literature is my major.
All the way from her ashes, she showed up by my side.

Hard to say what I'd been like before becoming a graduate.
For a decade I'd been a TV man, directing documentaries.
Kind of fancy job. It had pleased my parents and relatives.
I'm still wondering why I quit. Cannot answer it straight.

Let me reflect my two-decade-ago undergraduate days.
I organized a student poetry club, called Transcendence.
Many poets-to-be came. The most notable was her presence.
Except her, everybody left so soon that I was in a maze.

I was always looking for good words to expand my poetry.
She was always looking for ways to be poetically wordless.
We admired each other's works. Always in all seriousness.
Later on, we began to share each other, even physically.

I was thinking about her death, while walking in the library.
She had killed herself while pregnant. That's what I heard.
She had ended up a literature scholar. And she had married.
I heard her spouse was a TV man. No idea about him, really.

Twenty years have already passed, since our last copulation.
We parted the next day, promising to each other no more meet.
She said, "You're like a boomerang. Now you're leaving my heart.
Yet, someday, you will fly back." Since, no more communication.

The poem she showed me when we parted is as follows:
"Everything passes at an equal speed, undramatically.
Unemotionally. Unfalteringly. Unlimitedly. Uncannily."
I recited it in my mind. Ahead, bookshelves were in rows.

Something told me to stop by a computer-search room.
Something told me to discover her academic publication.
It may be saved right here as her final identification.
As a thing to mourn her and to retrospect her doom.

Typing her name in a search box, I clicked the mouse.
While the search was on, I was looking back on my past.
No poetry in my TV years. And I'm now returning to it.
Married, got kids, and knew that one grows by keeping house.

I hit only one item: "Theories of Silence in Poetry."
"That is in the basement," said a librarian offhand.
Nobody was in the basement. Just like a no-man's-land.
Every step I took, I heard a voice: "This way, hurry."

I read her essay alone, sitting quietly in the basement.
"Silence lets a poem vague," she wrote, "and complex.
It is imaginative, indescribable, and a variable X."
"It reminds me," she also wrote, "of human sentiment."

Her thesis was ambiguous, though her logic was clear.
This contradiction made me feel dizzy and exalted.
Putting the essay back to the shelf, I slowly turned around.
And I saw her appearing gradually and coming near.

A few candles are burning on her small dining table.
She and I are at the table, waiting for another person.
He is behind the wall. And phoning his TV station.
His voice sounds like mine. And sounds like a riddle.

"May terrorism come again," he shouts on the phone.
"'Cause I want a fancy story! Nothing like terrorism!"
His dinner gets colder. Her eyes shine like a prism.
Her spouse keeps phoning. His voice is like a thorn.

Out of curiosity, I ask, "Why did you choose him?"
She breaks silence. "Because he believes in Truth."
A long interval. "Then can you?" I ask at length.
"No," she replies quickly. "That's why I love him."

Then she vanished. I was alone underground.
No more dining tables. His fury also perished.
"Transcendence, maybe," I mumbled and departed.
Everything was passing, as she had said, aboveground.

A Camel and a Camera

Memory is hunger.
--- *from* A Movable Feast *by Ernest Hemingway*

My senile-dementia wife disappeared at last today,
leaving her senile-dementia husband alone here.
She left alone, almost naked.
May be wandering around in Shinjuku or Shibuya.
Winter is getting harsher.
Night is no more young.
Yet she is out. Maybe dying.
I am still waiting in this room
without eating anything.
Cannot eat without her.

"Senile dementia is a beauty."
She declared last night.
"You also have to be proud of it."

"I don't know you."
I confessed at last.
"My wife died of hunger during the Pacific War."

Then she whispered.
"So did my husband. In Manchuria.
As a patriotic soldier, you know."

Then I replied.
"In 1945? That's the year we wedded again.
The year we started building this new Japan."

She continued.
"There is one thing I have not told you about since our marriage.
I am a camel. I came from the Sahara.
In 1945, a big caravan brought me here."

I replied quickly.
"There is one thing I have not told you about, too.
I am a camera. I frame everything neatly.
In fact, you are also my picture."

"The caravan leader folded my hind leg
and tied it hard on a freight train," she added.
"Some nights later, I was in a huge market.
Camels like me were everywhere."

"Once filmed by me, everything looks like a charming product,"
I continued.
"But I have never taken my self-portrait yet.
I don't know what my own face looks like."

"I know your face," she said.
"You look like the caravan leader who tied my leg."
Then she fell asleep, but I could not easily.
As I started sleeping finally, I felt her touch.

"Human beings are boring creatures," she talked in her sleep.
"They are not hairy at all."
"A camera should be slick," I talked in my sleep.
"Otherwise, well, no one would buy it."

Oh, I cannot stand this loneliness anymore.
Time to go outside and search for her.
One McDonald's after another.
One Starbucks after another.
No camel is found yet.
Everybody looks as slick as me.
Carries a fancy lens.
Makes this city so charming.

I should be starved now.
Because so is she.
Hunger shapes us well.
It did in the war.

Now I am in a marketplace.
My past looms up vaguely.
Yes, I have been here before.
More than half a century ago.
People were walking slow.
With their legs folded.
And tied fast.
Over those vast ruins.

I find a familiar shadow passing away.
Two humps on her back.
I cannot catch up, though.
She is going back to where she once belonged.
She needs more sand.
Sand hurts me.

Dawn is coming.
Time to go back.
To where I once belonged ---
To that bleak room, I mean?
Yes, we built this city.
Sacrificed our lives.
That is why we had no children.
One for all and all for one.

Time to go back and take off my clothes.
Time for more hairs and two gigantic humps.
Time to throw away my obsolete lens.
Time to fold and tie my leg and sleep my life away.

Appearances and Disappearances

There are boundaries, and we cross them always at some risk.
--- from Metamorphosis *by Ovid*

"Hey, kin ya pay me dis much, Mr. Lonesome Mainlander?"

She whispers,
while picking me up on the main street at night.
She opens her palm
and shows me her five slender fingers.
"If ya kin, I go ya place wis ya from now
and do evrytin ya want me do. Only tonight, OK?"
She chuckles.

I was only imagining a girl like her,
while looking absent-mindedly at a small black hat left on the asphalt.
Now, before I know it, she wears the very hat.
How old are you, I ask.
"So what? Ya leave dis island very soon, eh?"
How did you know I'm not a local, I ask.
"Ya face, Mr. Horny Mainlander."
She speaks with a local accent.
She does everything I wanted her to do in my room.
When I'm about to pay, she asks.
"Ya OKed me, cause I look like exotic local?"
Well, maybe, I say.
"I tink I am a local gal, but people say ma family not yet local.
Dey say we need moaa self. . . self-sac. . ."
What? Self-sacrifice?
She chuckles again and changes her subject.

"If ya want see me agin, come back tomorro to place we met."
What if I don't, I ask.
"Ya want know me more. So ya come back.
Ya so programmed."

She starts sleeping by my side.
Then, while I'm fast asleep,
she, with her small black hat on,
disappears.

Finally, this long dream ends.
I wake up absent-mindedly.
I open a yellowish curtain.
Sunny day, as always, and very hot again.
Somehow reminds me of Hawaii or Okinawa in summertime.
Absent-mindedly, I change my clothes,
have a breakfast,
and leave this messy room.

Only once a year,
the main street is being changed into a pedestrian precinct.
So, now, it is quite crowded.
Yet the air is still full of exhaust gas.
Tourists after tourists, as always.
Yes, I was like them last year, I mumble.
Why did I choose to live here?
Because I was tired of living "over there"?
Because the island life looked cozier?
Because I was moved by this island's tragic history?
Or just because I wanted an island girl?
Anyway, I may look more like a local now, I mumble jokingly.
And blush faintly.
A number of colorfully-dressed street performers
are trying to draw the attention of every passer-by,
dripping with sweat.
Somehow reminds me of Disneyland.
Just as the girl suggested in the dream,
I start walking up to yesterday's place.
Standing there is
a Cupid-like statue of the last queen of the ancient island empire,
who was jailed,
raped,
and tortured by the mainland government,
and finally forced to

disappear.

Then
I notice an old woman kowtowing alone over the heated asphalt,
facing the Cupid-like queen.
I stand in the shade
and watch her at a distance, still absent-mindedly.
"I'm really sorry, all the Islanders," she shouts suddenly.
"On behalf of my homeland, I mean, the so-called mainland,
I sincerely apologize to you
for what my government had done to this island
for a long, long time."
She gradually raises her head.
Blood all over her face.
She quickly looks down and bangs her face
directly against the asphalt,
again and again and again.
No passenger dares to stop to watch her,
except me and two other bystanders in the shade.

Then
an old bearded man in a wheelchair,
with a wooden sword in his right hand,
appears from somewhere and starts shouting to the old woman.
"Don't apologize, you bitch!"
Wearing an old military uniform,
he starts brandishing the sword at random to attack the woman,
but cannot hit her precisely.
I assume that his eyes cannot see at all.
He yells.
"My god! She's disappeared!"

The woman keeps shouting in tears.
"I'M REALLY SORRY, MY DEAR ISLANDERS!"
A small black hat places itself behind her back.
The man quickly shouts back, brandishing the sword desperately.

"WHO GAVE THEM WHAT THEY NEEDED TO MODERNIZE THEMSELVES?
IT'S US, MAINLANDERS! THEY SHOULD THANK US! DON'T APOLOGIZE, OLD
HAG! OTHERWISE, I WOULD KEEP CALLING YOU A TRAITOR!"

Finally, his sword hits her spine.
She collapses flimsily.
Blood starts looming up over her white back.
Still, she pulls herself together and cries to the queen.
"I'm. . . really. . . sorry."
The old man starts pushing his wheelchair recklessly
and going around the statue,
pleased at having finally caught his prey.

"Dey did da same parformance here yesday, did'n dey?"
One of the two bystanders says loudly.
No --- This pedestrian precinct is held only once a year,
I mumble in my mind.
"Yeah, dey did. Dey are marry, eh?" The other asks.
"Yeah. Dey had no daughter? She wasn' here las night?"
"Yeah. I came see her, not dem."
They drop several coins into the small black hat,
and disappear slowly.

The old woman keeps crying and apologizing.
The old man keeps hitting his sword against her bloody back.
I start wondering again.
About me and the girl and her parents.
Some may avoid wondering this way,
considering it as simply unproductive.
But I cannot help wondering.
Because it seems far more intriguing
than choosing or deciding.
Wondering makes me a man of dreamy quality.

Another night comes at last.
The old woman with a bloody face stands up
and dusts off her clothes.
The old blind man stands up and folds his wheelchair.
They are ready to leave now.

I approach them and look into the hat.
Yes, it's the girl's hat.
Some bills are in.
The same amount of bills as I paid the girl.
The old woman picks the money, chuckling.
And leaves the hat on the asphalt, like last night.
Again, I'm imagining alone in front of the same hat.
Waiting for the girl's same whisper.
If this hat could be metamorphosed into her again.
The next long dream seems already on.
I may be so programmed.
The two old performers start retreating
gradually into the dark, like last night.
Accordingly,
the whole Disneyland kind of thing on the main street
also gradually disappears.

"Hey, kin ya pay me dis much, Mr. Lonesome Mainlander?"

Tanka: I Am

I am a spider
whose dewy web is still
missing many
warps and woofs; yet
I am a master of myself.

I am a mist
who spreads gradually
far and wide,
while still searching for
a chance to confine myself.

I am a dove
whose favorite branch to
take a rest alone
was cut out, so I fly now,
still confused how to fly.

I am a tower
whispering to the ear of
a child sleeping
at my foot: "Look, kid,
how blue the heaven is!"

I am a shed
who remains to embrace,
silently,
the future of every thing
rotting solitarily in me.

I am a potato
who, peeled, is decently put
on a dining table,
though I still remember

the underground darkness.

I am a fine rain;
I won't chase anymore
those who scattered
away, because, look, here's
someone waiting for me.

I am a valley
who is misted slowly,
along with a memory of
a man who left me to be
famed beyond mountains.

I am a comb
sleeping alone right at
the back of a drawer,
dreaming the full-blown
hair I combed years ago.

I am a honeybee;
I have lost my own way
in this nebulous city
in the middle of going back
to a sunflower standing far.

I am mud
drying up with
a good number of
footsteps of the people
masking their true faces.

I am a pine tree;
now another poet comes
to see me, addicted
to my every sharp leaf
and its evergreenness.

I am a zero
who doesn't have anything to
add to other lives;
but I'm happy now, because
I don't give anyone minus.

I am a forest
who flourishes deep inside
of a newborn's mind;
as time goes by, maybe, I'll
be doomed to soil and wane.

Midnight Rainbow

He is a monster like everyone else but what do you do if you're a monster
--- from "37 Haiku" in A Wave *by John Ashbery*

[1]
Hard rain is falling down.
All over this small town.
Misty cold midnight.
Only a few city lights are on.

Unable to sleep well,
a woman is still leaning on a sill.
The window is left open.
She is watching the rain alone.

Her dearest daughter is gone.
Run over by a truck.
That was a rainy night.
Her kid was walking after her.

"I'll follow you, mother.
But please don't turn around.
Or someone will come down
from the sky to take me."

She didn't turn around,
till her daughter shouted far.
"Look up, mother, look!
There's a rainbow in the sky!"

She turned around.
Her kid was running, looking up.
The truck couldn't stop.
And she was taken away.

The woman is still watching the rain.
And is still pondering.
Her husband is downstairs.
Maybe still mad, she thinks.

He was mad at the truck driver.
But also mad at her.
"How can you forgive that bastard!"
He shouted over and over.

"Even he is a part of the universe.
Like you and me.
Hatred won't change a thing."
She replied in tears.

"You're a hypocrite," he yelled.
"What a coward!"
He may be watching TV now.
To calm his own anger.

She turns to the door.
I may be a hypocrite, she thinks.
"Am I?" She turns around
to question the misty night.

No answer from the sky.
"Because I turned," she says.
"The answer may be behind me.
Like that rainbow."

[2]
He is still mad.
No ear to lend to the rain.
He turns on TV.
Shown is a war cameraman's face.

The cameraman was killed
in an ongoing distant war.
The narrator says,
"This is how he looked when he died."

The cameraman's face is smiling.
And full of seams.
Various skins are sewn together there.
Like a collage of many colors.

"He saw various wars.
The first war was the worst.
His face was entirely burnt then,"
says the narrator.

"He was trying to take a picture
of a kid burning to death.
It was a great war-picture moment,"
says the narrator.

"Money and honor was close at hand.
But he hesitated.
Then he dropped his camera.
And managed to save the girl."

He survived miraculously.
But his face got unidentifiable.
One rainy night,
her father visited his hospital ward.

"My kid died now.
Thank you just the same," the father said.
"Her head skin is still OK, though.
I'll scalp it for you."

"The girl's skin was safely stitched,"
says the narrator.
"Since then, each time he faced
a similar picturesque moment,

he dropped his camera.
And missed money and honor.
The people he dropped his camera for
thanked him a lot, invariably.

And they donated their skins to him."
And the narrator adds,
"I would not drop my camera, though.
I'm a true media person."

The cameraman stepped on a mine
and died, smiling.
He was on his way to a rainbow
he had longed to take a photo of.

"Midnight rainbow is a myth
in this distant battlefield.
Nobody has seen it yet.
And no soldier believes in it."

The narration ends without unveiling
why he chased after the myth.
"Maybe no clue to that,"
the father says and turns off TV.

"Why did I watch such a program?"
He asks himself.
He knows why, though.
He doesn't want to admit it, that's all.

He watched it,
because the cameraman's original face
resembled what he hates:
the face of the truck driver.

His wife is upstairs now.
Maybe still awake, he thinks.
The hard rain starts to be heard.
He imagines a rainbow.

[3]
Hard rain keeps falling down.
Over this midnight station.
Some drunkards are staggering
on a dimly lit platform.

One of them throws up
over a young man's shoe and slumps.
A flash of anger in the youth's eyes.
But he tries to be calm.

He still remembers what he saw
and didn't see that night.
He saw a truck lunging toward a girl.
Right in front of him.

He could have saved her
without that instant hesitation.
She shouted, "A rainbow,"
which he didn't see anywhere.

Since that night, he has been
pondering why he hesitated.
"Was I an egoist? Coward?
Did I really have to save her?"

If I had not turned around
to find her in peril, he thinks.
The rain is getting less hard now.
A train is coming nearer.

Suddenly, he hears a voice.
"Turn around," it whispers.
He turns and finds a drunk in peril.
The drunk who vomited on his shoe.

The drunk falls onto the rail.
The train is coming to him.
Nobody seems to notice it.
Except the young man.

"Don't save that guy, it's dangerous,"
he says to himself.
But his body moves.
Now he is standing by the drunk.

The drunk is snoring on the rail
as if he were almost dead.
The young man holds him up
in the train's headlight.

The drunk's body is amazingly heavy.
Like a boulder.
The young man starts carrying him away.
And the train falls on them.

The young man turns around slowly.
The headlight blinds his eyes.
Seven colors flash in his sight.
"Change me," he mutters to himself.

He has no idea what he'll become.
All he knows is
that tomorrow will be a sunny day
for everybody else.

Pudding

With one more step ahead,
X-rays will hit me from every direction like burning arrows.
Yes, yes, just like this.

"Will X-rays hit our tiny baby, too?"
My wife pointed out her sixth-week pregnant belly.
Three years ago. In this airport.
She asked me anxiously, passing through a security scanner like this one.
She was worried, back then, about the risk of so-called molar pregnancy,
if my memory is correct.
Wait, is it? Then, what about this?
"What if our baby ends up like a rice pudding?"
How did I reply to her?
Maybe I only smiled back. Maybe did not say anything good to her.
Maybe my mind was somewhere else then.
Maybe because I was struggling, every single minute of those days,
to find the best ending for the story I have been working on for years.

The title of the incomplete story is *With One More Step Ahead*.
Its protagonist is a novelist who cannot finish his story yet.
His lifework. He is still searching for its best ending.
And his tiny kid's eyes look so mesmerizing to him.
"I can even see an ancient fish swimming there," he says.

With one more step ahead,
that security officer will approach me and touch my body.
Yes, yes, just like this.

"How come you don't want to touch my body anymore?"
She came to my study all of a sudden. Stood behind me and yelled.
That was midnight. A year ago. Our kid woke up and started crying.
"You don't know what love is.
You may be a sage of love in your story, but not in reality."
How did I reply to her? I don't remember quite well.

Maybe I only smiled back. Maybe did not say anything good to her.
I was writing that incomplete story then.
My lifework. I was still searching for its best ending.

Look at this officer's stroke over my thighs.
Nobody has touched them so gently for years.
Look at his arms. How long and sturdy.
I wish I could have such arms. Look at my arms.

Maybe I could have saved my kid from falling down back then.
Those long steep stairs.
The showdown came a month ago.
The kid was climbing them down alone. And stumbled.
Of course, I reached out my short, thin arm.
Touched the left leg, barely. But could not grab it completely.
The kid stopped on the bottom stair, stained by blood.
I held up the body. Slapped the face hard.
I saw an ancient fish disappearing from the mesmerizing eyes.
My wife was not near me then. She was in her lover's room.

Where am I going? Who cares about my destination?
Everybody is gone. Just like that fish.
My lifework is in this suitcase. It is not finished yet.
And nothing else matters anymore.
Everything is uncertain now.
Just shapeless like a pudding.

With one more step ahead, another world will start opening.
Even for a dumb criminal like me.
With one more step ahead, I will see another stairway.
A long steep stairway. My flight time has come.
Yes, I'm jumping now. Yes, I'm falling now.
Yes, yes, just like this.

Tanka: A Man and His First Newborn

When I mount
my baby on my flat chest,
my breastbones
start creaking quietly:
Daddydaddydaddydad.

On my baby's chest,
morning sunshine rhymes
so tenderly
together with its heartbeat
time after time again.

Something like a bluish
ancient clay talisman
looms in my sight
as I come feeling my
crying kid in darkness.

So fragile that,
with one careless hold,
so easily,
this soul will vanish; again,
I wash my baby in warm water.

A soundless circle
expands slowly in the dark;
its center is
the sound sleep of my kid
who's finally stopped crying.

I summon you,
my self, who shows some
antagonism
to my baby's non-stop cry,

to surrender and leave now.

Another dusk comes
as I hold my wife's hand
with nothing to say,
while she cries, "I'm a failure;
I can't breastfeed again."

As if she were a monolith
for my life, my wife stands
in a shroud of the dark
and I'm carving our kid's name
on her; am I dreaming now?

This weight makes
me imagine an anchor of
a ship whose route
and destination are vague:
my baby's flesh and blood.

Opening its fingers
gradually like a seaflower
swaying slightly
deep in a warm current,
my baby awakens at last.

A Woman Full of Water

You saw nothing in Hiroshima. Nothing. / I saw everything. Everything.
--- *from* Hiroshima Mon Amour *by Alain Resnais*

Midnight.
The center of the city is uncannily quiet now.
No more trams run.
No more cars go by.
Oddly, even no glimpses of passers-by.
The baseball stadium looks like a big haunted house.
Each department store looks like a tanker
wrecked at the bottom of the sea.
Seems to me that only we are living in this city, I say.
Without saying any word,
she looks up at the top of the A-bomb Dome.
The full moon is shining above it.
Midnight.

Off limits.
The Dome is surrounded by a tall black fence.
"I wonder if you can climb this and jump into the other side," she says.
"For what? We may be reported to the police," I say.
"I wonder why you have to have a rationale for everything," she says.
And sneers.
She suddenly flies like a bat
and lands on the inner site full of rubble.
"If you want to have my body, come here," she says.
Her scent is seductive.
Her lips shine lusciously.
But I hesitate.
I check the sign again.
Off limits.

Millions of cicadae.
They start chirping

at each branch of each tree in the Peace Memorial Park.
Their lives will end shortly.
But they don't seem to care.
Sultry night.
City lights go out, one after another.
She starts stripping down.
Right on the old ashes of the dead.
Moonlight exposes her everything to my eyes.
I still hesitate outside of the fence.
I'm still afraid of the alarm system.
Darkness begins to shroud her flesh.
I get jealous of Darkness.
Millions of cicadae.

Common ground.
Between her and me.
Both of us were born here in Hiroshima.
The same skin color, the same hair color.
The Dome was a commonplace ruin for us,
not a mecca for sacred prayers.
The Park was just another playground for us,
not a solemn arena for tombstones.
We were taught to imagine realistically
what the hypocenter had been like at that moment.
Besides, both of us are chronically insomniac now.
Common ground.

Differences.
Between her and me.
She hates our national language
and wishes to perfect her English and Esperanto.
I have no intention to learn any foreign language.
She cares about humanity.
I care only about those who care about me in this city.
For her, life would be nothing without digressions.
For me, life would be nothing without repetitions.
For her, passion means sex.
For me, passion means art.
Surely, we need each other.

Differences.

The blast of moonlight.
She throws her clothes to me
and lies at the center of the Dome, face up.
I think I'm sleeping now, she says.
I wish I could have been alive at that moment;
I wish I could have watched the bomb blasting overhead, she says.
Now death is so skillfully hidden in this country
that I cannot experience any true terror here, she says.
All I have is hypocritical words and nothing original, she says.
The blast of moonlight.

Mixed emotion.
I want to make love with her,
because I have never gone to bed with her before.
The way she looks up at the moon over there infatuates me.
The way she dauntlessly seduces me over there
almost transfigures my entire system.
At the same time, though,
I cannot forgive what she has said right now.
That echoes like an insult to this city's history,
to this city's dignity,
to world peace,
and to me.
Mixed emotion.

Someone in the dark.
A drunkard? No.
Not only one, but some.
A bunch of homeless men and women? No.
Faceless people.
Bodiless people.
Millions of people.
Each one of them is a part of the whole Darkness.
Darkness starts raping her.
She still looks at me.
Her lips ask: "Isn't your name Hiroshima?
Isn't my name Neverland?"

I still hesitate to go in.
I may be able to save her, only if I try.
But I cannot try easily.
Darkness excludes me, and moonlight evades me.
Someone in the dark.

Kono onna no karada wa mizu darake dana
(This woman is full of water), Darkness says.

Kore de youyaku nodo ga uruoseru kamo shirenai
(She may be able to quench our long-standing thirst).

Sore ni hikikae
saku no mukou ni iru ano otoko wa
nante yakutatazu nanda
(Compared with her, the man standing behind the fence is simply useless).

Doko nimo mizu nado nasasouna karadatsuki janaika
(He seems to have no water inside of his body).

Shikashi (But)
kono onna no karada wa mizu darake dana.

I still hesitate here.
The copulation escalates.
Right before my eyes.
Holding the top of the fence, I read the sign again.
Off limits.
My emotion is still mixed.
Moonlight remains to blast over her body.
Darkness ejaculates at last.
The cicadae stop chirping all at once.
She starts to sleep alone at the center of the Dome.
No more trams run.
No more cars go by.
Seems to me that only we are living in this city.
I want to sleep, too.
I wish I could begin to forget all about this now.
And ---

I still hesitate here.

With One More Step Ahead

What is done out of love always happens beyond good and evil.
--- from Beyond Good and Evil *by Friedrich Nietzsche*

Doctor, Doctor, don't doubt me anymore.
Don't treat me like a piece of shit.
You know what, I'm not crazy.
People say I am, but that is not correct.
I don't need to be hospitalized.
No, I don't need you.
All I'm saying is I'm not the original, that's all.
I'm just a translation.
My original is somewhere else.
The translator is also somewhere else.
I don't know where they are.
Why should I?
I'm just a piece of translation.
Trust me, I'm not mad.
I should be rather called "systematically" mad.

Do you think that the language I'm speaking right now is my own?
--- Oh, you're a bastard, Doctor.
Don't forget that I'm a translation.
My original language is entirely different from this.
However, I still can't figure out what my original one is.
Isn't this sad?
--- Yes, Doctor, exactly.
To tell you the truth, you're a translation, too.
Did you know that?
--- Oh, you didn't?
Your original language may be the same as mine.
Isn't it funny?
Yes?
No?

83

--- Oh, you're wondering.
Haha. Hahaha.

Until when must we continue to speak this language?
Why can't you tell me what our original one is?
Aren't you a Doctor?
Aren't you wise?
--- I know I'm asking you too much at a time, son of a bitch.
Why can't you understand any language other than this one?
Why do we have to talk forever in a foreign language like this?
Why do I have to be your patient like this?
What's going on here?
Explain to me, you asshole.

Sorry, Doctor. I apologize.
I know my words are sometimes dirty.
It's not my fault, though.
It's my original's.
I'm a translation, you know.
I'm only repeating what the original already said.
You may say a translation is often different from its original.
You may even say
what a translation says is often not written on its original.
That is the case of a bad translation, Doctor.
A good translation like me has no distortion.
My husband used to say so.
Are you listening?
Doctor? Hello? Hello?

You know my husband?
I'm sure you do.
--- You don't? Well, whichever.
He was a poet. And he was a translator.
He is not dead yet. He is still alive.
He can't move anymore, though.
All his muscles are numb except his eyeballs.
But he can still talk with me.

Through his eyeballs.
If he turns them round once, it means yes.
If he turns them round twice, it means no.
If he freezes them in the center of his eyes,
it means that he is still wondering.
That's our conversational style.
Only ours.

He lies on the bed in his room, every day and night.
He can't breathe by himself.
A big respirator is set right by his side.
After that awful accident, his neck was surgically cut open.
A rubber tube was inserted into the hole.
My 24-hour job is to check if the respirator functions regularly,
to give him liquid food,
and, if phlegm clogs his windpipe,
to draw the tube out of the hole
and clean up his throat quickly
with another tube I personally call "the vacuum."

Will you call a person like him a vegetable?
Yes?
--- Well, then, call me a mad vegetarian.
Call me a systematically mad vegetarian, please.
Some people say I became insane, because he turned out like that.
Some say, because I lost my kid.
Others say, because I lost both of them suddenly
and got shell-shocked.
They are all stupid, don't you think?
--- Oh, thanks for saying yes. I'm losing neither of them.
My husband is still here. So is our kid.

He had been a hard-working poet, until our kid was one year old.
His poetry had been all about me and our kid.
He often said nobody would appreciate his works
except for us two.
He could not write about any other subject.
Some may say his creativity at that time was very narrow.

I don't think so.
I always loved his poetry.
Who cares about others' responses?
But he suddenly stopped writing poetry.
And started that translation.
And, afterwards, my kid fell.

Do you know the poet whose works he used to translate?
Cosmo is the pen name.
The real name is unknown.
So is the sex.
The poet still lives on a small island
where it rains under a completely sunny sky
and daytime comes together with nighttime.
"Sometimes a peace activist,
sometimes a child molester,
sometimes a terrorist,
and sometimes a parasite.
Maybe saint, maybe not.
Race unknown."
That's how my husband used to describe Cosmo to me.
I don't know anything further.

"Cosmo is like the Wandering Jew,"
my husband used to say.
"You know what that means?
Long time ago, a Jew insulted Christ and refused God.
Owing to this sin,
this Jew was destined to wander alone around the globe.
Is said to be over 1800 years old now.
In the medieval times, many people used to witness this Jew
and report to numerous lithographed newspapers.
You can still read them in some museums.
Maybe Cosmo.
Maybe not.
Well, whichever."

I don't know how my husband found Cosmo's poetry.
He was really into the poet, anyway.

I could not read the poet's original language,
but he had no problem at all.
Now I'm oblivious of which language it was.
I'm a dumb translation, you know.
My original must be programmed to be that stupid.
Maybe the creator of my original was a misogynist.
My husband used to tell me that Cosmo had no tongue.
Cut it off with a knife, voluntarily.
Because it would ruin the beauty of poetry.

"Cosmo's poetry is uncanny," my husband used to say.
"Always, something thematic is missing.
It has no substantial content.
It is just a form.
But haunting.
Cosmo's poetry can be read easy, but somewhat slippery.
Like a cake of soap.
But everybody needs soap, right?
So, everyday, I read each work again and again.
Cosmo's poetry is always about a father and his kid,
but treats them, always, as if they were nonexistent.
Uncanny, really.
No one knows who Cosmo is.
Here, there, and everywhere."

Nobody knew my husband's poetry, either,
except me.
My husband didn't publish his works.
He didn't need to.
He was writing only for me and our kid.
--- Wait, are you asking me how we were making our living?
Yes?
No?
--- I was making money, not him, Doctor.
I'm also a poet.
A professional poet.
Have you read my latest poem?
It is entitled "With One More Step Ahead."
It is not completed yet.

I'm still writing its sequel.

--- Are you asking me why my husband stopped writing his poetry?
Good question again, Doctor.
To tell you the truth, I'm not sure.
He once said this way:
"Look at this kid's eyeballs.
I can see an ancient fish swimming there.
How can I describe what these eyeballs are telling us?
My poetry cannot cover it precisely.
Because those eyes speak more than our tongues can."

My husband was thinking seriously
about the publication of Cosmo's poetry.
He was trying to have a good ending for his job.
But he couldn't after all.
As you know,
when he was about to finish translating Cosmo's final poem,
he fell from those stairs.
Those long steep stairs.
He was trying to save our kid from falling from the top.
Trying to grab the leg.
He couldn't.
And fell with our kid.
Lost all, except his eyeballs.
Cosmo doesn't know it.
I can't reach Cosmo yet.

My husband used to call himself Oblomovic.
You know what it means?
Yes?
No?
You don't know?
"Oblomov is an old Russian novel's protagonist.
A lethargic man.
Indulges only in eating, loving, and sleeping.
I'm just like that."
Not quite, I should say.
Because he stopped touching my body as soon as he knew Cosmo.

He was really into the poet, Doctor.
He lost the eroticism for me.
He resembles you, Doctor.
Ah, your face.

Doctor, Doctor, something strange is going on in your office.
Is this room really a sickroom of your hospital?
Where are your medical appliances,
other than this bed, this desk, this TV,
this radio, and that huge respirator?
Why does this room look like a study?
--- Wait, I vaguely know a room like this.
My kid's room?
My poem's protagonist's room?
My original's room?
Cosmo's room?
Or my own room?
Well, I'm mad, Doctor, you know that.

Today, I'll tell you the truth about my husband.
Nothing but the truth.
I'm mad, but not a goddamn liar.
I always tell a true story.
I always tell what has happened.
And tell what might have happened.
Well, whatever.
Today's truth is simple.
My husband stopped touching my body.
But my kid didn't.
So Cosmo became my lover.
I was longing to eat up the kid.
Like a cannibal, you know.
We almost became one.
And my husband became terribly jealous.
So he dropped the kid.

Yes, I wanted to eat up my kid.
The whole body. You know why?
--- Oh, you're so uneducated, Doctor.

You're a moron.
Can't you answer any question but the yes-or-no type?
Oh, silly boy --- Now, let me tell you why.
Because, if I eat, my kid's growth will stop.
Will remain the same until the end of the world.
My kid won't be ugly.
Won't end up like us.
My kid's beauty, aesthetics, whatever you may name it,
will be eternal.
Once digested in my belly, my kid will be reborn in my womb.

My husband didn't care about us.
With a sympathetic look, he often told me about such well-known miseries
as the bomb in Hiroshima or the massacre in Auschwitz.
But he couldn't love his nearest people.
Very often, his words were superficial and insubstantial.
He had missed an essential education.
He never listened to me with all his heart.
He was always busy defending himself.
He saw our kid not as his kid, but as his tool.
A tool to yield his goddamn inspiration.

He couldn't read our kid's eyes very well.
Not so well as I can.
He sometimes said its eyes were fishy.
Said they moved like the devil's advocate.
I said no.
I said they were the perfect mirrors of its emotions.
No distortion.
I said they were the perfect translation.
He said no.
He said they were distorted.
Said the kid's true self was one thing, while these eyes were another.
He couldn't read our kid.
Plus, it didn't matter to him.

He saw our kid just as an idea.
An idea for poems, which he didn't own.
That's why he even worshipped our kid.

Treated it as if it had been his own father.
The kid was the Word for him.
That's why he hated it at the same time.
He could not catch up with its sacredness.
He wanted to lose his own tongue and be like the kid.
So he jumped. Jumped with our kid.

--- Are you guessing that he was also trying to save our kid?
Yes?
No?
Which?
I can't hear you, Doctor.
--- Who said that?
Oh, no way.
I'm sure he didn't do such a thing, Doctor.
He is a murderer.
But, thanks to the murder he had committed,
he finally came back to me.
Now he is my kid.
He won't go anywhere, anymore.
Touches my body all the time.
All over my body.
With the help of my hands.
You can also do it, Doctor.
Look at me, I'm naked.
I'm all naked.
Look.

I like your speechlessness, Doctor.
You hide, I seek.
You hide, because you like to be found.
Yes?
No?
Which, Doctor?
Are you getting tired?
--- Hey, is this the right attitude as a Doctor?
Aren't you a responsible person?
It's getting harder for me to keep communicating with you.
Are you afraid of me now?

I need you, Doctor. Don't I?
--- What?
Who said that?
The next time you behave like this, I'll kill you.
Killing you is damn easy.
With my impulsive pull, just like this, you'll simply fall.
See?

I'm a translation, Doctor.
My original is somewhere else.
I'm a good translation.
Because I have no distortion.
The translator was a genius.
He erased his own shadow **perfectly** out of his **text.**
Due to his absence, I'm perfectly present.
And mad.
I love him.
He's a poet, too.
He's disappearing, though.
Like an ancient fish.
Do you know where he is going, Doctor?
Maybe you don't.
Because you don't know what love is.
You may be a sage of love in your poetry,
but not in reality.

Do you think he still loves me?
Yes?
Do you think you would love me if you were him?
No?
Where are you going?
Can you hear me?
This is like calling from the ground control
an astronaut disconnected from his spaceship
and floating aimlessly in the cosmos.
If you go, take me with you.
Retranslate me.
Recreate me.
Let me recreate you.

We were almost making it, weren't we?
Now you're about to leave me here.
Draw my hand, will you?
Otherwise, I wouldn't give this tube back to you.

Oops, Doctor.
Something is terribly wrong with your respirator, isn't it?
It's beeping, isn't it?
Doctor, can you hear it?
Can you hear me?
Hello? Hello?
This reminds me of my husband, Doctor.
Where is "the vacuum," for God's sake?
A vacuum.
Our vacuum.

Only you and me in a vacuum, how's that?
Let's play a game.
Let's feel this vacuum for a while.
Without moving at all.
Let's hush together, and have a wild thing.
Alright?

One hour has passed.

One day has passed.

Now how many days have passed?

No more beeping.
Nobody has come here yet.
Just two of us in this vacuum.
And this smell of rot.
I'm falling like you did.
Let's call it sleep.
Cosmo. Oh, Cosmo.

Look at me.
We can be genuine husband and wife.

However ephemeral we are.
Which of us is a husband, or a wife?
Who cares?
We'll be completely one,
with just one more step ahead.
We must find a good ending.
We must.

Goro Takano was born in the city of Hiroshima, and is an assistant professor in the Faculty of Medicine at Saga University, Japan, where he teaches English and Japanese literature. He obtained his M.A. from the University of Tokyo (American Literature), and his Ph.D. from the University of Hawai'i at Manoa (English/Creative Writing). His first novel, *With One More Step Ahead*, was published by BlazeVOX in 2009.

Made in the USA
Charleston, SC
12 February 2013